31 Ways To Promote Your Business, Online and Off

by Carol Bremner

31 Ways To Promote Your Business, Online and Off

How I view my business is best described by a quote taken from the book 'The Martha Rules' by Martha Stewart: "You will care about quality in a world where quality is often declining. You will listen to your customers in a world where that business value is often ignored. You will be a respected expert in a world that is overflowing with information but deficient in reliable sources of the 'best' advice."

Here are 31 ways to promote your business and expertise:

1. Creating Your Website

I often take it for granted that every local business has a website. The reality is that a large percentage still don't have an online presence. Recently, the Cambridge Times carried a column written by the advisor of the Waterloo Region Small Business Centre. The title was "Website a Must for Business" and Roy Weber, the author, likens not having a basic website today to being without a telephone.

That's a powerful example. Would you ever try to run a business without a phone? Even the companies that are too busy to provide personal customer service at least have an automated system that answers some of their client questions. But many consumers today go straight to the Internet when they want to find a local business or service. Without a website, you don't exist to those people.

A basic website can provide information regarding hours of operation, location, answers to frequently asked questions. Add topic related content and a way to collect the names and email addresses of potential customers. Now your website becomes a means to interact and keep in touch with those people. Your target market has given you permission to ask what they would like from you, to send them announcements, even to sell to them. All for less than the price of a coffee a day. Include social media in your marketing plan and your customers become your tribe and look to you as the expert in your field.

Ask yourself the following questions:

- What is your target market? Local only, or would you like to expand your reach and share your expertise using online methods? For example, a veterinarian in Vancouver not only treats local animals, but has a membership site to teach people all over the globe how to properly care for their pets. Those members gladly pay a monthly fee for the information.

- Do you want a blog connected to your website so you can interact with your potential clients regularly?

- Will you get traffic to your website using organic search engine methods or Pay Per Click?

- What methods of advertising are you currently using? Offline? Online?

- Are you listed in Google's local search at google.com/places?

- What keywords do you think people will use to search for you on Google? Have you checked at freekeywords.wordtracker.com or Google Analytics to see for sure?

- Do you have an opt-in form on your website so that people can sign up to your mailing list? Is it visible right away and does it require confirmation (this is called double opt-in)? Why would someone want to give you their name and email information?

- How do you plan to use your mailing list? For a regular newsletter? To send blog updates? To send one time announcements? To send an informative series? As a membership model?

- Do you currently make use of social media? Which ones – Twitter, Facebook Fan Page, LinkedIn, GooglePlus, Pinterest, Youtube, Tumblr, bookmarking sites? (too many to list them all and more coming out daily)

- Do you have social buttons on your site so you can easily be followed?

If you've been putting off marketing online, don't wait any longer. Promoting your business on the Internet is like driving a car. Once you start, you'll wonder how you ever managed before.

2. Domain Name Tips

One of the things I've noticed a lot of business owners do is to set up a free blog on Blogger.com or one of the other free hosting services and then neglect to register a domain name of their own for the blog. So instead of being able to tell people to go to carolbremner.com, for instance, I would be telling them the Internet address is carolbremner.blogspot.com instead. Not nearly as professional sounding. And when the price of domain names today is less than ten dollars a year, not a very good business decision. Following are some tips for registering your domain name:

- Your domain name should end in .com whenever possible. Don't use .info endings. Those are often used by spammers since they're cheaper, so Google frowns on them and you won't achieve good search engine rankings.

- Domain names are not case sensitive.

- It's better if the domain name is short, easy to spell, easy to remember and easy to say. The longer your domain name, the harder it will be for people to remember.

- No unusual spelling of domain names.

- Don't use numbers as part of the name unless you register both the written version and the numeric. Example: motivated2learn.com and motivatedtolearn.com.

- Brand your business with a name that describes it. Are there ways to incorporate keywords in the domain name that will be easy to remember? For example, for a web site that is marketing greeting cards, try to include "greeting" or "cards" in the domain name.

- Make sure the name isn't too limiting or silly. Best if it's a domain name that is short and easy to remember. Although most of the great catchy names like Google, Yahoo, Ning, or Twitter are gone, use your imagination.

- The name of your company may not be the best choice for the domain name. Your focus is on the products you have to market, not on the name you have chosen for your business. When someone does an Internet search for your product or service, they may never have heard of your company. But when they search for keywords that are part of your domain name, they will find you. That doesn't mean your website header has to be the same as your domain name. You can put your company name at the top of the actual web site.

- Visitors will associate your URL (website address) with the types of products you are marketing.

It will be much easier for your target audience to find your web site when using a search engine such as Google, since the keywords in your domain name indicate a relevant topic match. For example, if my domain name was fishing.com and a person typed 'fishing' into Google, my site would be a likely match.

- Register all forms of your domain name: I had the pleasure of listening to a well-known female Internet marketer. At the end of her presentation, she mentioned her website, Blogging4Boomers.com, so I went to BloggingForBoomers.com to check it out. Similar name but different site. And I found a totally different person running a website on a similar topic. Now that little mistake has probably cost this marketer a lot of money.

- When you register your website domain, consider any other spellings and register that name too. And if your site ends with .ca or .us, consider registering the .com extension as well. For instance, I have a site called CanadianWelcome.ca, so I also registered CanadianWelcome.com. Then I pointed the .com address to the .ca. Now, if anyone types in the .com URL, they will still be taken to my site.

- It's easy to forward a domain name to another site and saves you the grief of losing customers. Or even worse, having someone ask a lot of money to surrender the other possible form of your web address.

3. Steps To Register Your Domain

Domain names will cost you about $10 a year. Be ready to buy when you search since domain agents will often purchase the name if you don't and then try to sell it to you at a much higher price. My choice for domains is either Netfirms or GoDaddy. Others may be cheaper, but usually have a separate charge to keep your contact information private. With privacy, if anyone does a WhoIs lookup on the Internet, they will see your registrar's name and address rather than your own.

Once your choice of domain name is accepted, you will be asked for credit card and contact information to complete the purchase. If you have a Paypal account set up, you can pay with that rather than a charge card. After registering a domain name of your own, you have a few choices for hosting your website:

- Not recommended: Host a website with the same company that your domain is registered with. Although this is an easier option to begin with, it isn't the best. When I first started on the Internet, I looked for hosting services that offered free domain names as a customer bonus. But I found that if I didn't like the hosting service – one was way too slow to make changes on my site, another raised their prices quite a bit – then it was difficult to transfer my domain name. A costly lesson learned by trying to save myself a few dollars.

- Build a website using a free hosting service such as Blogger.com, or Weebly.com. Most services allow you to create websites without any coding knowledge.

Free hosting is a good alternative for people starting out who want to see if there is demand for their product or service. Some of the free hosting sites have small ads displayed on your site in return for their service. All of them have domain names that end with their company information. For instance, if you wanted your web address (URL) to be 'guitar lessons' a free site might be 'guitarlessons.weebly.com'. Not very professional and it's a pain to have to tell people that long name each time.

How much better to have the domain name 'guitarlessons.com'. When you register your own domain name, you can do that, even with free hosting. If you registered the domain name 'guitarlessons.com', you can set it up so that every time someone types in 'guitarlessons.com', they will automatically be re-directed to your Weebly site. That way, you can give people just the .com address and can promote your site as 'guitarlessons.com' on all marketing material.

- The third choice once you have your domain name is to go to a hosting company such as Hostgator and pay for hosting. I pay about $10 per month and that allows me to host unlimited websites. Then it's a matter of telling your domain registrar the location of your hosting so that they can be joined together. Your hosting service will give you two numbers starting with NS and you simply type them into the appropriate boxes on your domain name account where it mentions your DNS number. Within 24 hours the match is completed and you should be able to see your website on the Internet once you've added a little content to it.

4. Setting Objectives

What are your objectives concerning your website? Since I have a number of sites, I found it very helpful to write down my Internet plans for the year. Try to focus on your main objective for each site and decide on any regular features to incorporate. For instance, with my Internet Marketing site, my objective is to journal my progress as I create information products and as I set up my first membership site online. In the past, I've written about a number of things related to Internet Marketing with no real focus on specific topics.

Provide regular weekly updates about your business - anything that your target market would find interesting. Answer frequently asked questions.

Why not create an editorial calendar for the year? The calendar will give you specific ideas about what to write on your website. It isn't meant to be rigidly followed, but helps keep you on track. Write about other things as well, but this gets you started.

A calendar will list a lot of special days, such as Secretary Day. From there, brainstorm topic ideas. That way, each week of the month you can start with an idea and expand on it. For instance, one of the days mentioned was Red Day. Red got me thinking about bold colours, which got me thinking about image. That ended up as a topic about 'how to get your site noticed'.

5. Does Your Website Give a Sense of Security?

When a potential customer arrives at your site, he may be very interested in your product or service. But because you are a stranger, there is some apprehension about making payments to you online. What if you aren't who you say you are? What if the product is inferior? How can a person feel safe and secure doing business with you on the Internet?

I was reminded of all these doubts the other day when my husband was searching for a product online. He found a site that had exactly what he wanted and at a great price. But was it too good to be true? How could he be reassured? The business seemed to be in Vancouver and there was a contact page on the site to submit questions. But there was no exact address and no telephone number. Had there been merely a street number, it might be just a postal box. We were hesitant and ended up leaving the site without buying anything.

The next website we found selling the same product was a little more expensive. But many features at the site encouraged our trust. A telephone number we could call, a secure site insignia, the full address and email, testimonials from satisfied customers, and a guarantee.

That first business was probably fine, but taking the time to add those little things that created a sense of security as a buyer were what we were looking for. Whether you sell a product or a service, keep those points in mind and attract more customers on the Internet. Keeping customer security in mind can result in clients from all over the country.

6. Why Use Email Marketing?

An opt-in form on your website that collects the names and email addresses of potential clients offers a quick and easy way to keep in touch with your target market. By allowing you their contact information, these people are giving you permission to tell them more about what you offer. Used wisely, email marketing is useful for every businessperson.

Autoresponder services such as Aweber provide a number of different graphic web forms that in many cases have increased the number of people who sign up for email. By testing, you can see if a more visually appealing form makes a difference in your subscriber rate. Aweber has also upgraded their response messages. When someone gives you their name and email address, no longer do they simply get a text message telling them to confirm their subscription. Now the messages can also be audio or video.

Using an autoresponder allows you to contact potential clients with the click of a button, no matter how many subscribers you have. There is no better way to keep your business in the minds of your target audience.

Keeping up with a regular newsletter to your email list isn't easy, but I've found a shortcut that works for me. I have an online curated newspaper (content is my own and others and is automatically gathered) through www.paper.li and for a small monthly fee, I can take the html code when my weekly paper is published, add my own short message under the title, then copy and paste the code into my Aweber service and an informative newsletter is sent out with little work on my part.

7. Capture Customer Names

I've mentioned how important it is to have an opt-in form on your website. That way, when a visitor leaves your site, you still have a way to keep in touch with them. No matter how good your visitors' intentions, they will often forget you.

I was reminded of that fact the other day when my husband and I went shopping at our local lighting store. We found a set of lights we liked and were prepared to purchase immediately. But one of the fixtures wasn't quite the same colour as the others, so the saleslady said she would hunt up the matching light. In the meantime, why not go have a bite to eat and come back later?

Well, we took her advice and left to grab some dinner. But guess what else we did? We stopped at another store to check out their lighting. And we found another set of fixtures we liked that were on sale. So the second store got our business instead. All because the salesperson allowed us to walk away.

Our neighbourhood lighting store only had a few competitors and we knew exactly how to get back there. But we didn't. How much more crucial for you to capture your potential customers' information before your online business is lost in a sea of competing websites.

Take a look at your website. Do you have way to gather the names and email addresses of the people who visit your site?

8. Keeping In Touch With Your Customers

You know how important regular newsletters are to keep in touch with your customers. But finding time to write is the challenge. Sure, you could hire a ghostwriter, but it's best to write your own information whenever possible. After all, no one knows your business like you do.

I've tried sending a newsletter out every week and actually kept it up for almost a year. Then I ran out of steam. But because I use Aweber, I can still keep in touch with my subscribers on a regular basis. I have a schedule for posting to each of my blogs and have Aweber set to send out an automatic broadcast every time my blog is updated. Not only that, I have Aweber linked to my Twitter account, so a tweet is also sent mentioning my new post.

Although I'm still interacting, I've been feeling the need to send a newsletter on a regular basis as well. Weekly seems to fit my schedule best and since the blog updates are sent too, should be enough. I mentioned in point 6 that I've started using Paper.li, but you can try the following method instead: Write a few months worth of content at once, then load it all into an email provider and have the newsletters sent on schedule. That way you can write everything once and forget about it for awhile.

Thanks to programs like the Aweber autoresponder, it's now easier than ever to contact the people that are interested in our products and services. How do you keep in touch with your clients?

9. A Clear Call To Action

When a potential client visits your website or your place of business, what do you want them to do? Buy something? Sign up for your mailing list? Visit your business location? Without a clear idea of what you want to happen, it isn't easy to give a clear call to action.

Even when the desired outcome is clear to you, do your customers know exactly what you want them to do and how to do it? Ask yourself "If someone walks through my physical or virtual doors, are they guided along the marketing path I want for them?"

Silly question maybe. But on a visit to Chucky Cheese with my family, it wasn't clear what we should do. It's a restaurant, so we sit down and order food, right? Not so easy. It was a Saturday and the place was packed. Children and their parents were at all of the activities. We expected that, since I'd been there once before on a weekday.

What I didn't expect was the reserved sign on every empty table. There were eight of us and we were planning to buy food, drinks, and tokens for the games. After walking through the whole place a few times, we could not find an unreserved table. Was the place booked with birthday parties that hadn't arrived yet? We asked one of the employees if there were any empty tables. "We're really busy today" she responded. "You might find one near the back".

After twenty minutes or more of trying to find a spot to sit, we decided to leave. After all, more people kept coming and there were no tables. Or so we thought.

Once back at home, we told the rest of the family that Chucky Cheese had been too crowded. Not one table without a reserved sign. That's when my son told me what we should have done. Apparently, once you order your food, the reserved sign is removed from one of the tables and you are seated. I guess that keeps people who don't order food from taking all the seats. Even though those same people are paying for game tokens.

Sorry Chucky Cheese, your call to action wasn't very clear. If a hostess had mentioned the seating policy when she greeted us, it would have made a big difference. Or even when we left, if she'd asked whether we enjoyed our time. But now my experience has left me less than eager to visit again. Too bad, they missed out on a big order and we would have loved to give them our business.

Put yourself in your customer's shoes and walk through the steps. How can you make sure there is a clear call to action? On your website, where do you want them to go from the page they are reading? Have a clear menu for them to see and recommend what to do next.

10. Using Re-directs and Anchor Text

I often see business people use long, unnecessary links on their website content, in their emails, and when speaking about an Internet address. Three cases come to mind:

I was at a business to business networking event and a man promoted his new Blogger blog to the group. Its URL was thesitename.blogspot.com. Not too professional sounding. The same with sites that end with rogers or wordpress.com. There was a time when domain names were expensive, but not anymore. For under $10 a year, you can register your own domain name and then set it to point at your free website.

When using email, which sounds better: yourname@yourcompany.com or yourname@gmail, hotmail, or yahoo.com? Once you've registered a domain, you can use it to give your potential clients an email address that is a constant reminder of your company, instead of promoting a generic email service. Using a free address may cause customers to wonder if you can afford to do business properly.

Anchor text is a clickable website link that uses a descriptive phrase as the text. For instance, instead of a link that says 'example.com/mydirectory/pictures', using a link that said 'car of the future' and having it link to the longer URL not only looks much better, but lets the search engines know exactly what that link is about.

Often your site will receive better search engine rankings as a result, meaning it will be easier for your target market to find you. The same applies when sending an email that has links to various areas of your website. Use anchor text for a cleaner, more professional image.

Now take a look at your marketing materials. Could your copy be helped with the use of domain re-directs or anchor text?

11. Search Engine Spiders

Search Engines have a little program they send out to websites to "crawl" or "spider" each site picking up information to index in their search results. You optimize your website pages with keywords that, through your research, you feel will bring in traffic. Next, you place the keywords throughout the text on the page, without making your content difficult for a person to read. Your main goal, after all, is still good, solid content for your readers.

Your chosen keywords or keyword phrases should be mentioned in the title of your page and in the first paragraph, then sprinkled throughout the rest of the page. The search engines will pick out your keywords using their robots, bring them back to their computers, index you and give you a rank based on a number of factors.

12. Re-Purposing Your Content

As business owners, we spend a lot of time creating content – for presentations, websites, marketing pieces – any number of things. Why not re-purpose that content and let it work for you in many different ways? Although Tip 31 goes into more detail, here are my favourite ways for keeping my content in front of people:

- If your blog post is over 250 words, post it on an article directory such as ezinearticles.com for extra exposure. Your bio and a link back to your site will be there and when people take your article to post on their site, a whole new market will be exposed to your expertise and you'll get more traffic to your site.

- Turn your written content into audio and upload it to your site. Using freeconferencecalling.com you simply talk on the phone and your recording is available as an mp3 download for you to use.

- Create a Youtube video similar to the text content and link it to the original.

- Take video or audio of your presentations and sell or use as marketing material.

- Try out Blog Talk Radio and use the resulting audio on your own website as well as on BlogTalk and in iTunes.

- Create an information product and have it available as a digital download, a CD or DVD, even a physical book.

13. Website Technical Support

I host my websites on Hostgator and really like their service. For example, when updating one of my sites, all of my content suddenly disappeared. After my initial heart failure, I went straight to the chat feature for Hostgator's tech support. There were two people in front of me in line, but my wait was less than two minutes.

I quickly typed my problem into the chat feature and the technician looked at the problem. Less than a minute later, my site was back to normal. There had been a problem with the WordPress database and he had repaired it. Then he took the time to explain to me how to fix it myself should it ever happen again.

With my former hosting service, I had to send an email if there was a problem and wait a day or so for the answer. I love the fact that I can chat to a Hostgator support person whenever I have a problem. I have a number of websites, all hosted with Hostgator for a low monthly fee. Add that to their excellent customer service and it's no wonder I recommend them whenever I can.

As well as needing good technical support for your own website, think about how you can add a chat feature or some kind of excellent support service for your customers to use.

Update: After years of satisfaction with Hostgator, they have been purchased by a large corporation and the quality has suffered. I'm once again wondering about whether I should change hosting. Part of me thinks I should and the other part hates the thought of moving all my content somewhere else.

14. Listen To Your Customers

I've been researching options to create a membership site and have narrowed my choices down to two – one a monthly fee and the other a one time payment. I was leaning toward the former and emailed them to ask the differences between both programs to justify the extra expense.

I received the following answer: " It would be great if you will be a part of our community, so that members of this community will know what are your ideas and be a part of your connections. Interacting and sharing interest can contribute a lot from exposing yourself and all that is about your own community. We are happy and excited if you will join our network. Our membership site is a big community it will help you a lot in building up your own network."

I don't know about you, but I can't understand this email at all. It hasn't answered my questions and the poor use of English has me worried. It's too bad because I really liked the sounds of this company before I received their email.

Try looking at your customer service from a patron's point of view. Are you closing the sale or closing the door?

15. Provide Excellent Customer Service

When working online, excellent customer service is even more important than it is in the offline world. Your perspective clients can't see you face to face, hear the way you speak, or judge your body language. Those are all decisions that come into play when someone is deciding whether or not to do business with you. No matter how good your company's reputation is, if you or your salespeople come across as arrogant or rude, you'll lose a sale.

So how can you make a positive impression on the Internet? Well, there are a few ways that will keep people coming back to find out more about you and your business. You can add audio or video to your site. That way, customers begin to feel that they know you. At the very least, have a photo of you and some background information on an "About Me" page of your site.

Another important matter is making sure you respond to comments left on your site or emails sent to you as quickly as possible. If in the past you've provided efficient customer service, they may be willing to give you another chance. But if a first contact isn't responded to at all, not even with an automated follow-up message (easily done with an autoresponder) you'll leave a negative opinion of the company. Even when the service you provide is excellent, without excellent customer relations as well, your potential clients will lose interest!

16. Customer Service - Does It Set You Apart?

When a person walks through your door or uses your service, do you become memorable to them? Do they tell their friends about your business and sing your praises? Or are their comments negative? In these days of social media, experiences are shared with hundreds of people and you risk losing more than just that one customer. How can you make your customer service amazing?

I'm one of those people that will allow poor customer service without voicing my displeasure at the time. But I will never use that service or go to that establishment again and will tell everyone I know to stay away. When I encounter excellent customer service, I come back again and again, bringing others with me. Competing on the basis of price alone could never produce that kind of loyalty.

Excellent customer service is what will keep people coming back week after week. Businesses that are spotlessly clean and attractive, employees that obviously enjoy working there. Staff that do their best to make their customers feel special. Little things like notifying them when a shipment comes in, to the big things like making sure that when a person arrives with a complaint, they leave happy. As a result, people will tell other people and new customers will come.

That's the kind of customer service we want. Satisfied people telling others on social media or at their jobs about what a great business we have and how highly they recommend it. That kind of feedback does more than thousands of dollars spent on advertising.

17. Productivity and Outsourcing

As a business owner, how do you keep up with the many little tasks that threaten to eat up all of your time? One way is by outsourcing. Hire a Virtual Assistant and use her as your executive secretary. When I get behind with my writing or I don't have time to learn the technical aspects of a task, I call my V.A. She can get a sales page uploaded and a payment method installed while I'm still wondering what to do first. And when you find a good Virtual Assistant, hold on to her. There is no better person to have on your team.

There are other methods to help your productivity, some free and others paid services. The key is to automate as much as possible. Use an application such as Hootsuite to quickly keep track of your Twitter, Facebook,, LinkedIn, and Google+ profiles all in one place.

Set your autoresponder to send out update notices to Twitter and to your mailing list whenever you update your blog. Use a small address book to quickly retrieve your passwords. Set up folders in your email account to quickly sort your mail if you can't act on it right away. And keep gathering productivity tips from others – there's always room for improvement.

18. Coaching Using MP3 Recordings

There is a coach in England who has found a way to work with clients from all over the world and in many different time zones. She creates tailored podcast tutorials for her clients to download as MP3's they can listen to whenever they want to. Are there any other ways you could utilize this idea for your business?

19. Youtube For Business

Many business owners have realized the power of video. For instance, an enterprising artist was having trouble selling her paintings. So she started taking videos showing her creating the painting and discussing how she got her ideas. Then every week, on the same day and time, she posts the video on Youtube with a link under it to the eBay sales page where she is selling the painting. Every week she gets more viewers and her paintings sell for more.

Now that GooglePlus has been added to the mix, when you post on Youtube and have it connected to Google+, it will automatically appear there too!

20. Google Research

Google is one of the best places online to find out the needs of your potential customers. Try typing a topic name, the plus sign and the word 'forum' and you will find out what consumers are saying about various topics. For example: dogs + forum will get you a list of a number of different forums that deal with dogs.

21. Host a Meetup

Would you like to meet some of your potential customers offline and get to know them? Or want to present some information about your product or service? Why not host a meetup?

Start by going to Meetup.com and register your new meetup. You'll be charged a small fee and they will help publicize your event. You decide on the topic, the location, and any fees attendees will pay. That's it. Within hours, people who are interested in what you're delivering will start to register for your meetup.

22. Free Traffic From Television

I once appeared as part of a three woman tech panel on our local Rogers television station. I was there to answer questions about blogging and my blog address was displayed every time the camera was on me. It resulted in extra traffic to my site for a number of days after the show.

The community television station in your area is usually on the lookout for interesting guests and features, so why not contact them and offer to share your expertise with their viewers? The fact that you are a local resident will also work in your favour.

Although you won't make any money by appearing on one of their shows, the publicity that results will bring people to your website. If your business is new, you will also become known as a resident expert.

23. Host and Record a Teleseminar

Did you know how easy it can be to record your own teleseminar or teleconference?

First, go to freeconferencecalling.com and set up an account. The service is free, but you and each of the people involved in your call pay long distance charges. For those participants without long distance plans, Skype allows calls from a computer to a land line phone for a very small fee.

You'll be given a phone number and a special bridge number that belong to you alone. Use that number over and over again, whenever you like, and as often as you like. Up to 1,000 people can be in on the call, which can last up to six hours and be held at any time.

As the moderator, you'll be given a pin number that you'll need to use to activate the call. You can see how many callers are on the line, mute and unmute, and record - all with the push of a telephone key or two.

Once the call is finished, simply hang up and the recording stops. Then later in the day, login to your account at Free Conference Calling and the mp3 of your call will be there waiting for you. Calls are posted on your recordings page for 30 days and can be downloaded for use on your website or anywhere else you choose to keep it.

24. Keep Current

Reading summaries of current business books is one way to keep up with trends and information. There are many others, including reading the business section of the newspapers, various business magazines, and business books from the library or your local bookstore.

The price for keeping current is spending time, so you want your activities to count. I like to keep up with business and Internet practices by using the time that my brain would otherwise be taking a vacation.

For instance, I exercise on a mini trampoline set up near my computer. That way I can watch informational or tutorial videos while I work out. I download text from business ebooks to my ebook reader and read it whenever I have to wait – in line, at the doctor's office, etc. And I download audio podcasts to my iPod to listen to while I walk or do the dishes.

Whatever your method of keeping current, there will always be more information available than you could ever absorb. Part of being a life-long learner is deciding what you need to know and what you can safely ignore. How do you keep current in an ever-changing world?

25. Keeping Your Focus

One of the hardest things about conducting business online is keeping a clear focus. It seems almost every day I'm enticed by a new product that would make my online life much easier. If only these were junk advertisements, I wouldn't be distracted. But many of the offers really are helpful for building an online business. That is, if you have the time and energy to learn how to use them properly.

I hate to admit the number of times I've purchased products or services for my Internet business and then found I had neither the time or the skills to implement them. For instance, I had a webinar service set up so that I could do regular training online. But after six months I still didn't have the time to figure out how to use it, let alone market the training sessions.

On the one hand, we need to keep up with all of the new technology. On the other, we need to concentrate on those things that will build our businesses. A fine line, and one that I am still having trouble walking.

Update: after two years of putting it off, both because of time and being intimidated by the technology, I am finally using webinars on a regular basis and feel quite comfortable. But it had to be when I felt ready.

26. File Management

The beginning of a new year is the perfect time to organize your files, both physical and on the computer. Weed out all the duplicate or outdated information. Decide on a filing system that works for you. I've read a number of organizing books and have tried numerous filing methods. But I still haven't found the right one for me.

I tend to over-organize and end up with three times as many file categories as I need. Then when it's time to find a document, either on my hard drive or in my file cabinet, it takes endless searching. For instance, a report about Twitter could be in the Social Media file, or the Traffic file, or the Internet one. I could have duplicates in all those places, but for me it seems like a waste of paper or space to do that.

27. Mindmapping

Event preparation, product creation, and working on a new project – these all need a lot of thought and planning. One of the things I find most helpful is using a mindmap. I start by drawing a box in the middle of a large sheet of paper and writing my main topic inside. Then I draw spokes to sub-topics, then more spokes to sub-sub-topics, and on and on. If I forget a step, I can easily include it on the map.

For a computer based approach, you can go to Mindomo.com to see their online mindmapping software. If you are a visual person, try mindmapping and see if it simplifies planning for you. My productivity has really increased since I've gone from lists to mindmaps.

28. Create a Business Funnel

The best business clients are those who buy from us over and over again, not just once. Attracting potential customers online is no different and the easiest way is by using the funnel model to keep them coming.

The wide top of the funnel gathers buyers by offering low priced products or services. Then the funnel gradually provides higher priced items. Depending on your business, you may not be able to offer all of the levels, but the goal is to provide as many as possible. The following is a proven funnel business model with number one as the entry level and number five offering the highest ticket items:

1. Tell your customers what to do in a general way. For example, an overview of how to add memory to your computer.

2. Tell them how to do it step by step using text or audio.

3. Show them how to do it – video or live training.

4. Sell them a product that does it for them.

5. Do it for them.

If you have a product, create services to support it. If your business provides a service, create a product to match. Keep creating more products or services to offer.

29. Mastermind Groups and Mentors

This past year I've become more involved in mastermind groups and am achieving more success as a result. We meet for a weekly brainstorming webinar or teleseminar with the recording made available to listen to again. Then each of the participants post our goals for the following week to keep accountable. As the members work on our various projects, we get much needed advice and feedback from one another. All of this is done in a private and very supportive environment.

As an extension of this idea, members of your group could take turns commenting on one of the member's blogs, tweeting about them, promoting that group member whenever possible. Then the next week, those marketing tools are used to help one of the other people in the mastermind.

In the past two years I've also been investing in coaching and as a result, my business has grown. I've found that having someone to mentor me past the challenges that they've already navigated makes it so much easier for me to move forward and make good choices.

30. Twelve Tips For Trade Shows

I had my first trade show booth at a local women's show held twice a year. It was a busy, exciting time and I learned a few things in the process:

- Wear comfortable shoes.

- Make sure you have plenty of water since you'll be talking most of the time.

- Have large print visuals. It seemed a lot of people liked to examine from a distance before they decided to approach the table.

- Smile and speak cheerfully. Not easy when your feet hurt, but necessary.

- Don't cross your arms, especially if you're standing up. It sends an unfriendly vibe to people.

- Stay behind your table, unless you're giving out treats. I found that some people acted as though I was about to pounce unless I sat behind the table.

- Some people won't be interested. Instead of wasting time trying to convince them they need your product or service, realize that not everyone is your target market. Then focus your energy on the few that do want to hear more.

- I don't know about you, but I hate pushy salesman. People love to shop, but they hate to be sold to.

- Try to keep conversations at your booth off to one side so that people can still see what you have on display.

- The most popular booths were the ones that allowed potential clients to be involved in some way. How could you interact with the people who stop by?

- Think about the type of people who will be attending before you commit to a trade show booth. For instance, a show for seniors probably wouldn't bring you many possible clients if your business was a nightclub. Or a show for new moms might not be the best venue to attract business coaching clients.

- Have fun – people will be attracted to your enjoyment.

There you have it. Twelve things I've learned as a new exhibitor. I did have fun and I'm looking forward to the next event I can be involved with. It was a lot of work, but I contacted about sixty potential clients. All in all, a good use of my time.

31. More Ideas For Re-purposing Your Content

Now that you may be considering re-purposing your old content, what does that really entail? You can re-use articles, blog posts, ebooks, press releases, social networking posts, forum questions you've answered, videos, audio files, interviews, books, reports, notes from seminars, and blog comments made or received.

Consider ways to re-purpose *before* you create projects from now on -- not afterwards. What are your potential clients' preferences, favourite communication style ("voice"), favourite format (video, tips, eBooks, etc.), level of expertise, needs, complaints, challenges, and requests to you?

Also consider what's been written before on the topic, what's currently hot, if the content is evergreen or if it might become dated. What hasn't been covered on the topic and what different angles or different slants could be used to re-purpose your work? Think about current news stories or topics found in magazines. Is there a way to explore the topics from another angle or in a creative new format ideally suited to your subscribers?

Why not outsource, particularly for product creation areas that would require time for a "learning curve" if you were to produce a specific format yourself? Outsourcing methods could include video or audio creation companies or specialists, transcriptionists, ghostwriters or copywriters. Outsourcing can save time and make you money, if used wisely.

Re-purpose your content to match your subscriber's level of expertise. Also consider the predominant learning style expressed by your audience:

- **Visual** (pictures, videos, diagrams, charts)
- **Auditory** (MP3 files)
- **Kinesthetic** (prefers to "do" as they follow along with instructions)
- **Linguistic** (prefers text)
- **Unique** (e.g. members of or dealing with a differently-abled group such as those affected by ADHD, autism, visual challenges, etc.)

Your old content can be compiled or broken down into the following formats:
Screenshot videos, Live videos, MP3 audio recordings, Email courses, Press releases, Articles, Blog posts, Guest posts, Ezine ads, Expert interviews, Short reports, Free or bonus reports, eBooks, eReader books, Physical products from digital ones, Transcriptions, Social Media posts, "How to" courses, Advanced lessons, Intermediate lessons, Beginner lessons, Slide shows, Work aides (templates, checklists, etc.), and PowerPoint presentations.

Re-purposed content isn't saying the same thing several different ways. Why create information for a one-time use, or in only one format? Always be looking for the "extra twist" to boost the value of what you share -- and its ROI. Begin today, and make re-purposing your content a natural, lucrative and labor-saving part of your business goals and strategies!

I hope you enjoyed these 31 Ways to Promote! Come visit me online at carolbremner.com for more ideas and tips.

www.ingramcontent.com/pod-product-compliance
Lightning Source LLC
Chambersburg PA
CBHW060934050326
40689CB00013B/3091